MOTOR DISTURBANCE

A Frank O'Hara Award Book

KENWARD ELMSLIE

Motor Disturbance

PUBLISHED FOR
THE FRANK O'HARA FOUNDATION
AT COLUMBIA UNIVERSITY PRESS
New York and London, 1971

Acknowledgment is made to the following publications in which these poems first appeared: *Adventures in Poetry:* "Chinese Creep"; *Angel Hair:* "Duo-Tang," "Feathered Dancers"; *Ant's Forefoot:* "The Old West"; *Art and Literature:* "The Dustbowl," "Flaming Creatures"; *Best & Co.:* "Jan 24"; *C:* "Another Island Groupage," "Florida Hillocks," "History of France"; *Juillard:* "Satie for Two"; *Lines:* "The Verandahs"; *Locus Solus:* "Experts at Veneers," "Shirley Temple Surrounded by Lions"; *Mother:* "Dirge"; *Paris Review:* "Japanese City," "The Power Plant Sestina," "White Attic"; *Telephone:* "Small Soda," "Terrific Afternoon"; *University Review:* "Great Eastern"; *Wagner Literary Magazine:* "Fruit"; *The World:* "Fig Mill," "Gene Pool," "Junk Fish," "Larry's Savvy Wad," "Motor Disturbance," "Night Soil," "October 29th," "Single"; *The Zodiac:* "Permanent Heyday." "Pavilions" and "Donnybrook Fair" were published in *Pavilions,* Tibor de Nagy Editions (1961), and "Island Celebration" first appeared in *Power Plant Poems,* C Editions (1967). "Girl Machine" was published in a limited edition by Angel Hair Press (1971).

FOR JOE BRAINARD

THE 1971 FRANK O'HARA AWARD FOR POETRY

The annual Frank O'Hara Award for Poetry, named for the American poet who was killed in 1966, was established by the Frank O'Hara Foundation to encourage the writing of experimental poetry and to aid in its publication. The award is meant to carry on in some measure Frank O'Hara's interest in helping new poets in their work. Eligible for it are poets who have not had a book of poetry published or accepted for publication by a commercial or university press. Further information about the award is available from the Frank O'Hara Foundation, 145 West 45th Street, New York, New York 10036. Columbia University Press, for the Foundation, published in 1968, *Spring in This World of Poor Mutts,* by Joseph Ceravolo, in 1969, *Highway to the Sky,* by Michael Brownstein, and in 1970, *North,* by Tony Towle.

The winner of the 1971 Frank O'Hara Award for Poetry is Kenward Elmslie, who was born in New York City in 1929 and grew up in Colorado Springs, Colorado, and Washington, D.C. In 1950 he graduated from Harvard College. Two pamphlets of his poetry have been privately printed: *Pavilions,* Tibor de Nagy Editions (1961), and *Power Plant Poems,* C Editions (1967). Two collaborations illustrated by Joe Brainard were published by Boke Press: *The Baby Book* (1965) and *The 1967 Gamebook Calendar.* Black Sparrow Press published his long poem, *The Champ* (1968), and *Circus Nerves* (1971), a collection of poems, both in limited editions. Kulchur Press issued *Album* (1969), a collection of stories, song lyrics, short plays, and poems. His theatre works include three librettos published by Boosey and Hawkes: *The Sweet Bye and Bye* (1966) and *Lizzie Borden* (1967), both composed by Jack

Beeson, and *Miss Julie* (1968), composed by Ned Rorem. He has also written the book and lyrics of a musical play, *The Grass Harp,* based on the novel by Truman Capote, with music by Claibe Richardson. Mr. Elmslie has won a Ford Foundation Grant and a National Council on the Arts Award. He lives in New York City and in Calais, Vermont.

The design for the jacket of the clothbound edition and the cover of the paperbound edition of this book is by Alex Katz.

CONTENTS

MOTOR DISTURBANCE

WHITE ATTIC

The white attic rests
among dripping trees

with unrolling tunnels
and trembling luggage

around were dens
all kinds of dens

and dazzling fruit
to weary the wind

the sun would end
and we'd smoke among the trees

our wary arms
tenderly relaxed

the urn faces a tree
of unequal height

when it came I grew
moved to two rooms in town

where I reach out at night
and bat the far air

1

EXPERTS AT VENEERS

"In Montana, claws skim through the dawn,
herders just saddle up, yes that's it!
But then, they gulp hiccough pills in the highschools,
not to skip one ambiance in the tunnel of fun."

That symbiosis in the garden says to adventure.
The jelly on the daffodil will mildew by July,
and the orange result if the birds come by
will suffice as our capitol, won't it?
    And I was there, and I was there.

Here we are, in what seems to be an aerial predicament.
The Government certainly looks handsome in the mackerel sky,
awaiting wind fungus, beribboned in its way, goodbye.
Blackamoor stump, how luminous you'll be.
    And I was there, and I was there.

FLORIDA HILLOCKS

the fecund plantation
the damp areas of the squatters
the valuable ocean bushes
seed pearls in the ancestral mouth safe
    drop noiselessly in the apron

follow this guilty yellow instrument
bury it in the orchid swamp
out of insane attic windows
prophetic widows will gesture
    put jonquils — crotches — haunches —

the winter garden above the gazebo
is suffering from cellar blight
awful mushrooms spell out our names
oranges in the river squeeze against the piles
    jewelled hirelings have stolen all the gates

bugs attached to strings (our toys)
form immediate mosaics
of roses drying, of the boy's pillow,
of lithe janitors, of seed pearls dropping
    down the well of the fecund plantation

FLAMING CREATURES

From the tug the shore crops are merely blurry wilderness
much as in chase dreams of dogs, stones have smells
volatile as cities in a holiday mood
where getting on and off platforms cones the night's events.
We on the tug recall death in the trees,
parachutists gliding down to mined branches, all seen in mirrors.

The Narrows was the end of our white adolescence.
The Mauve Shadow, the whale comedian,
flicked over surfaces all its own,
with membranes like balloons left in the sun,
in search of a shrivelled event, or shrivelled events.
The stewardess says in an outfield (it)
a recognizable fire was lit.

4

FRUIT

Oranges,
someday the Negress who smears you with certified color
will hear tap-taps and whines (the Giant Fruitbeast) in the swamplands
arising like natural music, and she will shriek in her swoon
"American youth, go stomp on your car graveyards!
Small boys in acid underwear, once more you may yoo-hoo
at trains in the night. Whoo-ee, the alleys of Kansas
are now devoid of yellow joke eggs that hop peep and explode.
City children, accept the perfume of your melons in the sun —
Lemons."

Limes,
in spring you remind some men of little people's breasts.
Irish bodies — the huggle-duggle of many cellophane sacs —
or even the Indians on stilts who harvest government orchards
know: a lime on a turntable encourages the wrong voyagers.

Plop them into snowbanks, northern strangers, and in summer
when they roll onto roads, slovenly families at pasture
will remember to kick the cattle. Farm women in bed a-mornings,
think of them in your bureau, then get up. A nation of you and you,
Grapefruit,
Tangerines,
could only prove the all-nite cities have won. O lovely spring,
the carnage! Oldsters with blinky chicken eyes resent your seeds,
your sections, your juice and meats. Secretly in markets,
they pinch you, hurry on and sniff their fingertips, estranged.

PAVILIONS

1.

        Maddened
the city fathers stalked out of the legs-on-legs section of *Vesuvius!*
(two days long — how *moderne* — but the ballet outlay!
Plus the problem of the rest of the electorate's summer,
everyone's anxious children, fanning their own brown legs on the porches,
the influx of minorities from the hills,
the constant danger of great truck garden, fruit and berry spoilage —

("Get out the mobile units. Get out the mobile units.
Gather the interesting busses,
let them coincide with the subway where it lifts itself into the sun
and there in the racetrack garden annex,
we will walk through the parlor-car exhibit

        no, we will not rap on each window at any nice flamingo
        no, we will not hold up food to make them follow
        a banana one window, a chicken leg the next,
        no, we will save our picnic for the sleeping-car exhibit,

and when we feel ourselves start to move through the night,
we will walk on and simply take off our clothes,
our berth is our home,
for we will know, parade,
we can always summer here!")

and still the unconscionable snow eddied under the sill
onto the sampler quilt on the mining couple.
      "Take off your lamp, Fred."
Pesky annunciations every storm: what was sewn and what snow?
Each gust altered swirls — gists —

                    he who is spilt
                          windows in June
                          turn to mirrors in Jan

                    like milk in mid-air
                          windows in Jan
                          turn to mirrors in June

                    can build flowers of moonstone
                          mirrors in Jan
                          turn to windows in June

                    and still despair
                          mirrors in June
                          turn to windows in Jan

spoke to her much as crust flakes
matted in the leg-hair of the Norns
(arranged like doves, all of them on the bronze and copper labyrinth)
spelled out to those members of the audience with binoculars
emphatic messages of grave personal joy

                    decipherable
                    that afternoon

                flowers, flowers
        we accept the temperament of the landscape
                    unlulled by false lilts,
        head cocked for the whirr of any aerial knives
                        pinwheeling in from the coast,
        open to the resonant barrage of the moment

                    decipherable
                    that afternoon

                flowers, flowers
        we accept St. Rita eating ashes
                    to her hands, warmed-up feathers.
        Emergency, emergency in the mountains!
                    So. Rocks also accurately limn
        the hot stomach of any god who singes

                    decipherable
                    that afternoon

                flowers, flowers
        we accept the sleazy manœuvres of those who scent out
                    our childhoods, trussed in white tulle,
        moaning away in something tub-shaped, thrashing:
                    spastic replicas of old hysterias,
        musty old musak lanterns tap-dancing through the landscape

                            8

                    decipherable
                    that afternoon

            flowers, flowers
we accept circling in the inside of a shell, alone,
                    pawing through grains, insect-like
with many careful feet (ossified seed, where are you my love?
                    I must carry you off to the country of the sun)
only to come across — vanished, my one complementary presence!
                    — warm and telltale ashes

                    decipherable
                    that afternoon

such emphatic messages of grave personal joy
a sawmill couple holding hands on a bench
at rest after sharing a candybar,
unaware a climax of lava had alchemized
doves into white stone figures,
sensed some newly oblong aspects in their sweet city,
                    trees too cooled by the sunset,
                    a stillness of silent autos baking.

2.

That was that calm winter but that was that summer the wharves collapsed,
that was that summer we always call our hoosh summer,
yes — hoosh, hoosh,
because mother made us stews
and our elbows stayed cool,
         heh heh.

O yellow latticework and diamond-shaped pieces of blue sky days
zestfully I lay back, zestfully. Then some more back,
dear sweet dancer, forgive this dirty old man,
that was that summer of my first great pleasure spirals.
Looky! Girls in organdy bloomers on my lawn, *my* lawn,
my first eurhythmics!
Have some cookies, girls,
hey someone look lively,
those bicycles are falling, first one, the next, another,
a regular party,
plop plop — too late now!
They're drifting downstream.

That was that summer of my tiny vision. Golden balls, silver balls,
minuscule, raced about the floor like witty animals
giving sportive chase, and all while I was shitting.

That was that same final summer, not very violent,
of the many couples on stilts
who dinner-danced and dinner-danced, skeletal but fond.
That was that summer I not only bled and bled on my pin-up of Mt. Etna
he spluttered (stop the car it's rolling backwards forwards which?)
that was that summer
it's us the earth turning, us I thought,
him the white sun speeding
back into the beauty of a parlous blue clarity,
not them the clouds, not them the clouds, moving
that interesting fall.

3.

The bogus couple sprayed their bonus verandah of steel net-mesh
with mahogany, maps, and a little wire studded in places.
             Aztec dinner-dance tonight
came through the tube just sprayed with granitic follicles
to deter the youngsters from inhaling so much.

What of their home? The garden spray had finished wetting the wall
and now was drenching some flowers and a rainbow.
             Aztec dinner-dance tonight
came through the tube as Aunt Grass sprayed it
with putrid motes to deter the family decadence: random sniffs.

             Olé, the floating islands
             managed their pavanne
tastefully bumping like vague turtles.
             Some strange mountains
             lumbered into the garden,
languidly embraced while night parrots moaned.

             A silly atmosphere
             greeted Mt. Popocatepetl.
Then the forgivable rush of pine surfaces, avid,
             sparks and gashes,
             the pain of new chasms in the zodiac.
They sprayed a little, and hummed around the red ruins.

"That was the best spray of them all, dumping ancient milk out the window."
She pulled up the covers (that's how she went): whirred into invisibility.

        Aztec dinner-dance tonight

came through the tube. And how she would have wanted it.
But what of our processions? South? Further South? South?

        No. Let us shamble back North. Back North.

        East and west lie black posts

            in a hot sky,

            guides anyway.

THE DUSTBOWL

The Harvey Girls invaded Kansas that spring of the famine
nudged by sweet memories of cornfields in the snow.
 Okie weeders. Stranded in the orchards. Huts. Silos.

Ah, the times they had — huts — racing down avenues
of rattly stalks, droopy and sere, oooo-eeee! roughhousing
 in jeans and poke bonnets until the laundry basin

 announced supper (thwacked) beans and jello (thwacked)
followed by coupling in the sheds. Alas that winter of the famine
 there were no sheds, and still they stayed, sullen

 girls of the south, squinting at yellow skies
out of verboten shacks. Alas that summer of the famine
 they breakfasted on leaves from gullies

 and the air tasted of acorns, ah, the meadows smelled of vanilla.
Alas that winter of the famine, their men lay down on the highways,
 and their women lay down with them, and felt the hot truck wind.

 Alas ladies in the cities, clutching their scalloped hankies,
oiled up the icy sidewalks in the violet dusk
 and hitching up their leathern garments, fell and sued.

14

Taxes. Caverns. Cereal. Vegetate. Simple gestures
(entering attics, bikes wobbling, dogs sunning)
    lurched into something checkerboard, with every piece

    outsized, gummed to attract the police.
The Harvey Girls slept until came the spring of the glut.
    Thrumming, the weed machines released an ebony menace.

    That summer of the glut, the fields were like monsters in heat,
and the Harvey Girls, freckled and worn, smiled at the northern mistral,
    and headed on mules for the mountains, that autumn of the glut.

DONNYBROOK FAIR

We mustn't zone our gold-star mothers,
tamp them into cavernous taverns,

or complain if banks gift them with tweezers;
nice folks are turned into chieftains with jaws

by the rigamaroles of gamblers and zithers.
Wracked winner-loser, wracked loser-winner,

gray colleens, the city's bewitched,
and only Mont Blanc knows a loss when it sees one.

Scotchman, arrange for our gold-star mothers
three things: a winch where the heather soughs,

a dune where willows drop slim leaves,
and a sunny arroyo of egrets and cows.

DIRGE

the inside of balloons is not cool
the other person always hears one walk (skree)
so many giant worries
the shredding process and wrapper consumption
can only be intimated from the arm that hands things in

white bread is another menace
if smaller balloons of forest scenes should float past
of Orkney visages and afternoons of golf
we could climb in 'em 'cept the blowers are malfunctioning
and refresh ourselves sniffing cowhides in the rain

arranging leaves and pleasant smelling filaments
to afford ourselves a temporary bower
which when shrivelled resembles a sentimental sediment
on a cushion of ready-made messages

the balloons are away obfuscating some enemy
at last we enjoy the city sky squashed as it is
between the itchy buildings crevasses and terraces
which are beginning to —
skree! bus fumes felled another human unit.

HISTORY OF FRANCE

Wind, cold, rain.
Then came the sky person:
a pale empress.

Today is beautiful —
such lively girls!
A sharp-cornered stone hovers.

Ah, rigid acceptance!
Money buys everything
except walls between people.

The empire in the rain
with the muzzled atmosphere
stopped us at the border.

Striped barriers! Oafs!
And beyond, men in swimsuits shout,
"Art, make us free."

Another plaintive morning
full of chickens, dust, and buoys.
The sea keeps re-beginning . . .

Lobster claws in the pine forests
betoken an illogical sea
which sings: I *know,* I *know.*

Sticky tar and plastic messes
clarify the alliance of judge and guide.
True democracy need never exist.

Not only need, but never will.
Think of cliffs. Think of peacocks.
And the salty skiffs of the colonels.

Withdrawing rooms come next — perfumed earphones
for the young people: it's the Divine Sarah.
Wooden leg sounds bump about the divans.

"Secrecy in the provinces,
a journey under a waterfall —
these won't test your manhood, Robert."

A pretty woodwind, and thrushes.
They say the dormers fly open
to admit sweet-faced aristocrats.

And the maids dump out the cakes,
the pretty bush designs on the main course,
while everyone hides letters in hollow trees.

The party includes the lady with the map-shaped face,
the boyish man, the chess-playing lifeguard;
how they love the French summers recently.

The cleverer towns have crested yellow parks,
nice and oblong with ferns and pebble deer,
and on these the old sweet lovers loll (the wasps).

Underneath them, musical flushing,
tunnels to the ocean,
and bloated hairy sea creatures.

We have never (bump) sat on (bump) rocks,
the women facing west,
and watched the Atlantic and Pacific sunset,

the men tucked into blankets,
the children tucked in too,
and the old people in the cars.

Well done! You see, the cities
have erected spangled circus nets
or are they nests?

Into them (keep whirring, pap factories)
ocean souvenirs fall, misty bitchy things,
so the boulevards get more usage.

20

Now, in the mountain gravel pits,
the workers wear scoopy hats,
in which they smuggle out the granules.

But in the mauve valleys,
such attractive colleges,
all built on animal cemeteries, alas.

In winter, they pack 'em solid,
come spring, to Hans and Ivan's amazement,
but now — he reaches the valuables:

fountains of exposed beasts and breasts,
lottery tickets in the sluices,
to prevent the acids from seeping through.

In the warehouses, racketeers
daydream of that sky person,
the pale empress.

At lunchtime, they take it out,
the tongue-shaped wooden box;
today is beautiful.

SHIRLEY TEMPLE SURROUNDED BY LIONS

In a world where kapok on a sidewalk looks like an "accident"
— innards — would that freckles could enlarge, well, meaningfully
    into kind of friendly brown kingdoms, all isolate,
with a hero's route, feral glens,
    and a fountain where heroines cool their mouths.

Scenario: an albino industrialiste, invited to the beach at noon
(and to such old exiles, oceans hardly teem with ambiguities)
    by a lifeguard after her formulæ, though in love —
"Prop-men, the gardenias, the mimosa need anti-droopage stuffing."
Interestingly slow, the bush and rush filming.

Hiatus, everyone. After the idea of California sort of took root,
we found ourselves in this cookie forest; she closed the newspaper,
groped past cabañas, blanched and ungainly.

The grips watched Marv and Herm movies of birds tweeting,
fluttering around and in and out an old boat fridge, on a reef,
when eek, the door — or was it "eef" — "Shirl" said the starling, end of —

The janitors are watching movies of men and women ruminating.
Then a cartoon of two clocks, licking. Chime. Licking, chime. *Then* a?
   After that, photos of incinerators in use moved families more than
the candy grass toy that retches. Dogs. For the dressers, *Mutations,*
   about various feelers. For the extras, movies of revenge that last.

This spree *has* to last. "Accept my pink eyes, continual swathing,"
Shirley rehearsed. "Encase me in sand, then let's get kissy."
   Do children have integrity, i.e. eyes? Newsreels, ponder this.
How slow the filming is for a grayish day with its bonnet
   bumping along the pioneer footpath, pulled by — here, yowly hound.

THE POWER PLANT SESTINA

Horizon, burn with a smoky flame.
Thousands of women will bob up and down
left, right, left; and right, left, right.
Give me something pearl-shaped and soft
(like blue crystals) to offset hard work,
and don't forbid amber at the center.

At the center,
fossils flame,
and resins work
like jungle rafts moving down
evil-smelling rapids so soft
the rubbery leaves above look "right."

How right
for embers at the center
steamy and soft
in an annual flame
to feel like down, warm down
on cheeks that never work.

Work, work. A world of work!
Dahlias! Zinnias! Give us this right!
"Detention" addicts, we bend down
and search for the center,
the glassed-in flame
that sifts tough from soft.

Terror makes us **soft**:
see how earthquakes work.
The example of flame
gives us the right
to choose the edge and abandon the center.
Watch it hurtle down!

Through a smoky sky, it'll hurtle down.
Instead, something pearl-shaped and soft
will reconnoiter around the vanished center:
blue crystals to offset hard work.
Feel all right? Feel all right.
Protected from flame? Protected from flame.

Down goes the flame,
soft-seeming and right
as the center of all work.

PERMANENT HEYDAY

Say we fall asleep entwined at nine
and the world is fine
then we wake up entwined at nine
and the world is much the same

ai-ee! those stains on your shoulder
remind me of favored South Sea islands
this marsh is so enjoyable to glide through
though my frozen tongue keeps sticking to your teeth

once you led me up clammy stone declivities
lugging a huge leaden replica of me
which melted in the phosphorescent rivulets of lava
beneath our mobile hut on the red volcano lip

I felt revivified enough to read war magazines
under trees that oozed in the blonde moonlight
a plug had been pulled — venturesome areas —
and the world is much the same

if authorities disown our witty free-falls
and great hectic crowds peer out of bathyspheres
would-be tourists to Atlantis — where are the stairs —
(they'd analyze your stains as a sunspot curse)

and if beautiful die-hards in rear-view mirrors
"proven" cases of blue giants beckoning
boil down to road ads rattled by traffic
(only some emblem confusion or other)

I'll think of the impact of spring and buzzing
the way pretty vines chip away at office buildings
frolics and thrashings in icy eddies
it's a natural mistake but observers believe

you know of jungles where diamonds explode
(the ones that relieve themselves on any swollen member)
leaving behind only valueless snakeskins
like envelope windows caught in bare city trees

ISLAND CELEBRATION

for James Schuyler

The overgrown roads around here refract water-and-mirror mirages.
The lakes, buffeted by winds from the south,
    are the bane of narcissists. All they see reflected are clouds

    boxed into rectangular segments with sky areas evenly in-between —
vistas as hyper-organized as those Chinese puzzle houses
    which make one too trembly to lift spoons past shoulder level —

    one is always secretly sloshing liquids into flower arrangements.
If only one could peer under the table to see who has the erection.
    Instead one hunts for the door to the moth center garden

    past the laundromat, the mattress room, the Wild West sauna,
(a mobile electric chair rushes by, emitting sparks, straps flailing)
    ah, the door, the handle — a stranger! Boudoir mirror. Oneself.

    The resultant dearth of energy leads to mole-like panics,
agitations and positionings in closets, or else one waits in brambles
    for semaphored advice from some person on a hill.

    Around here, all is simpler. Down the paths whistling minks
rush unafraid. Too clumsy to shy at the beauty of bodies,
    they never pay for the damage they do — trampled mushrooms,

28

bruised raspberries. And the storms never pay for the damage *they* do.
   Same with the map. All who look at it lose focus
and succumb to the montages of a tinselled mainland — Tinselled Mainland:
   midwestern swimmers exercising on flat garage patios,
   leaf decor smelling up incinerators — Halloween Dance o'er —
   stumped yellow and green passenger trains,
   many tufted balls rolling down national arteries.
The photos by the bed (notwithstanding some suspicious splotches)
   are harmless — seasonal changes arrayed in sequence:
rock to sludge, sludge to lichen, lichen to bracken,

   water onslaught, holes that gurgle and squirt,
tongued plants that billow like parachutes plummeting within a sea,
   and finally, the harvest, the stoppages, ice and wind.

   The person on the hill whose arms remain akimbo
is most likely not unlike oneself — if only proper stillness
   would occur. Tests, measurements. Cascading berries

   would render them useless. Same with the map. The actual elbow
of the beach is longer, crookeder, with grass like a colleen's bush,
   freckled and muzzled, and with fewer warm air spurts.

   In the portrait over the fireplace, the inverted green teacup
is the whole island, the pines too, 1912, two sisters on a picnic,
   armistices and solstices, with no trace at all of shattered glass.

JAPANESE CITY

Centennial of Melville's birth this morning.
Whale balloons drift up released by priests. Whale floats parade
followed by boats of boys in sou'westers jiggled by runners
followed by aldermen in a ritual skiff propelled by "surf" — girls.
In my hotel room with its cellophane partitions (underwatery)
I phone down for ice-water, glass, tumbler, and the cubes.

Cattle for the Xmas Market fill the streets.
Black snouts — a rubby day indeed. Bump the buildings, herds.
A Mexican seamstress brings back my underthings shyly
six, seven times a day. One sweats so, lying about.
She mentions marvelous pistachio green caverns
where one canoes through cool midgy Buddha beards

where drafts of polar air sound like cicadas, where —
About the partitions. The other travellers seem —
There were beautiful hairs in the wash-basin this A.M. —
thick, and they smelled of limes
(good, that jibes with mine — ugh! —)
but mine, how perverse! Form a hoop, you there. Mine,

mine smell like old apples in a drawer. Jim the Salesman
and his cohorts are massaging my feet — a real treadmill example.
They're in lawn decor, ether machines, and nocturnal learning clasps.
And Jim? Plays cards in his shorts, moves black fish around.
Black houses, the capitol. Hotel chunks. Sky chunks. The squeeze:
green odd numbers — white air, amputations and eagles, respite.

Red even numbers — body sections, the ocean sac, the great beach.
Green even numbers — oval jewels, quicksand, the haven behind the falls.
Jim's stammer is contagious, zen smut about hatcheries in the suburbs,
how the women in the canneries came down with the "gills,"
hence bathtub love-makings, couplings in the sewers. The ice-water comes.

The room-clerk's pate shines up through the transparent floor.
Soon the sin couples will start arriving, and the one-way mirror teams
and the government professionals with their portable amulets —
shiny vinyl instruments that probe and stretch.
Much visiting back and forth. Pink blobs. Revels and surveys.
Many olive eyes'll close in a sleep of exhaustion. More ice-water!

The celebrants in metal regalia jangle and tinkle
moving past the red-roofed villas of the Generals,
past the cubicles of the nakeds and into the harbor,
past the glum stone busts of the Generals, sitting in the water.
Out they go, (Jim etc.) into the sweet emptied city, leaving behind
the red odd numbers untouched: pleasure beaches, monsoons and sun.

THE VERANDAHS

discern in the smoky garden
              funeral after funeral
huge moth parades wind
              around window screens
best ignore the smell
              of the transient statues
and the live ones waiting
              to be scooped into the clouds

the terrace people are dizzied
              by extraordinary volcano displays
they compare claw marks
              up and down their bellies
the descent from cement
              city to sea city
has been accomplished
              by the fix-it apparatus

when we join them
              we will show them trophies of old smoke
shaped like them
              replicas of a menaced band

FEATHERED DANCERS

Inside the lunchroom the travelling nuns wove
sleeping babies on doilies of lace.
A lovely recluse jabbered of bird lore and love:
         "Sunlight tints my face

                and warms the eggs outside
                perched on filthy columns of guilt.
                In the matted shadows where I hide,
                buzzards moult and weeds wilt."

Which reminds me of Mozambique
in that movie where blacks massacre Arabs.
The airport runway (the plane never lands, skims off) is bleak —
scarred syphilitic landscape — crater-sized scabs —

painted over with Pepsi ads —
as in my lunar Sahara dream — giant net comes out of sky,
encloses my open touring car. Joe slumps against Dad's
emergency wheel turner. Everyone's mouth-roof dry.

One interpretation. Mother hated blood!
When the duck Dad shot dripped on her leatherette lap-robe,
dark spots not unlike Georgia up-country mud,
her thumb and forefinger tightened (karma?) on my ear-lobe.

Another interpretation. Motor of my heart stalled!
I've heard truckers stick ping-pong balls up their butt
and jounce along having coast-to-coast orgasms, so-called.
Fermés, tousled jardins du Far West, I was taught — tight shut.

So you can't blame them. Take heed, turnpikes.
Wedgies float back from reefs made of jeeps: more offshore debris.
Wadded chewy depressants and elatants gum up footpaths. Remember Ike's
"Doctor-the-pump-and-away-we-jump" Aloha Speech to the Teamsters? "The —

he began and the platform collapsed, tipping him onto a traffic island.
An aroused citizenry fanned out through the factories that day
to expose the Big Cheese behind the sortie. Tanned,
I set sail for the coast, down the Erie and away,

and ate a big cheese in a café by the docks,
and pictured every room I'd ever slept in:
toilets and phone-calls and oceans. Big rocks
were being loaded, just the color of my skin,

and I've been travelling ever since,
so let's go find an open glade,
like the ones in sporting prints,
(betrayed, delayed, afraid)

where we'll lie among the air-plants
in a perfect amphitheatre in a soft pink afterglow.
How those handsome birds can prance,
ah . . . unattainable tableau.

Let's scratch the ground clean,
remove all stones and trash,
I mean open dance-halls in the forest, I mean
where the earth's packed smooth and hard. Crash!

It's the Tale of the Creation. The whip cracks.
Albatrosses settle on swaying weeds.
Outside the lunchroom, tufts and air-sacs
swell to the size of fruits bursting with seeds.

ANOTHER ISLAND GROUPAGE

the bunks in the bogus square
twittered with skeletal birds
we ate the Spear People syrup pear
and listened for "twin" words

the past has gotten blurrier
insecticides ate up the sampler
Ganymede and his worrier
open onto (as if catapulted) an ampler

vista: gismo, curtain, gismo:
(gismo) pronouncing weedier "rothier"
(curtain) Alabama notions like Quiz Mo'
(gismo) the three mirrors of the clothier

and now angelic cranes must swing the maidens
into retentive and shadowy valley hugs
The Britishers in the Spade Inns
will take tea gingerly, muffling the "ugs"

manifested behind the curtain
after wither discussions (swans and swans)
they let the vigorous dirt in
the bonbons and herbs and second bonbons

bleary-mouthed they gulp the water
(girls in their mouths) nectar
and buy the partitions of the park daughter
metalling them to protect her

when tantrums are sung to motherly saints
(re the policy of the rain police)
a black rock avalanche repaints
the persiflage of the victim's Greece

DUO-TANG

Laundry so near the ocean bothered Frank.
The lack of medicine on the shelves
also confused his emotional stance.

A moth fluttered against his leg.
A gust of wind made his Pepsi keen
as its foam trickled down inside.

A banana boat on a horizon otherwise blank
passed over a time-piece buried in valves
over which sea-growths stirred. Grant's

Tomb. Cleopatra's Needle. The Hague.
He flipped the pages of the travel magazine
and wondered if Monsieur had lied.

Tomorrow, he'd go to the bank,
shop for some unguents and skin salves,
and finish the Castles' book on the dance.

The Hesitation Waltz! How vague
the past seemed: static scene after static scene.
He watched the retreating tide

and patted his belly. The sun sank.
Monsieur and J. were off by themselves.
He took off his pants.

He was too proud to beg.
He lay down and thought of Jean.
The sheet had dried.

JAN 24

for John Ashbery

take care keep in touch best wish for New Year
what'll it be: tango palace in banana republic

that's one of the luxuries of longish-term survival in NYC
thinking of smallness and walled-off sad little dumb little places

New Zealand was my first post-puberty country crush
how it welcomed me and my wonderful labor-saving devices

permanent waves strap-onable wings automats for the capitol
socialism I love you your housing weekends sandy-lashed settlers

first let me explain my "just room for one more" dread
picture book of World War I mounds of about-to-be-buried corpses

sub-sub-sub basement flashed by hours ago and still moving down
that fu manchu creep peering through the peep-hole is no super

judging from the lamasery teetering on the fez-strewn cornice
it's Albania and I'm to rescue poor dear dotty King Zog

milk-white victim hands are protruding out of the glacier below
hands that sprout bushy werewolf hair when the moon is full

electrolysis and gelatine capsules could keep these hands nice
the catch is the nation's lovelies'd grow freak mustaches

the clandestine crystal set lights up: you're #1 Commie, Anna
it's Roumania and Anna Pauker pushes off in the goat-cart

polemics polemics polemics she moans phuffle phuffle sigh
my first lady dictator whew that explains the butch hair-do

lucky she has me to brain the transmission key
in mid-enzyme-synthetic-organ-introjection hormone cycle

Anna wake up the transmission key is now smashed
Anna and Zog are playing bezique on the Blue Express

dance manual *pour moi?* Anna rests her scruffy head on his shoulder
a solitary tear wends its errant way skirting medal after medal

piranha are nibbling iron clouds above Tirana
their droppings — filings — scoot about the cobblestones

magnetized by distant word reverberations (memo: keep ears to ground)
back to Anna and Zog in their sumptuous berth (Praha München Paris)

see the green cube Anna in the mesh cooker unit
it's poking out its pterodactyl wings very over-soul, hein?

its beak is caught Anna says taking hammer from handbag
it's probing its feathers for social parasites like us Zog joshes

Papillons d'amour Anna says swooning into a spoon position
her first dirty joke and they awoke thus in a bus in the Rockies

just as this morning we awoke in a spoon position you and I
unfolded unthinkingly and dispersed for another time's up type day

41

FIG MILL

As to that lady hiding in the closet
("Spring is here!" "Spring is here!")

it's only February and spring ISN'T here,
not here in this western locality.

Rich in history and Indian lore,
the street names follow the Generals.

Which reminds me of a cowboy
who all his life was a model,

a loathsome cowboy in a mobile home
pressing against the glue-covered glass.

Surprised we haven't worn out our windowpanes,
windowpanes, windowpanes, using our binoculars.

This morning a flock of little pin sis-
kins flew in, the beautiful things,

made for the cool water,
and everyone took the hint.

and moved away from the drinking facilities
ing and bathing facilities.

One of our guests is an elderly man
we always refer to as the monkey.

He sits in an old armless rocking chair.
Anyone know how to take out the noise?

Always a crowd to see the portrayals!
Bearing the well-known bundle in his beak

a model stork made straight for the house.
A notice reads "NO MORE, PLEASE!"

He climbed atop this man's shiny bald head
as if to say, "Out of my way! I need a drink!"

His bright red bib
completed the fib.

Seagulls circled overhead.
Time for bed.

No tidbits there,
just dead air.

Candlelight and kisses sweet
ediblize the toughest meat.

I write poetry and song lyrics.
Bix, let me know if you can hear.

We'll form a chain of friendship
but I need suggestions please.

Flowers and/or birds painted on whip-
cord, chicks and chicadees

working away at a sunflower seed
in the winter-rusty green grass.

Now a history of Valentines.
A woman in Worcester, Mass. —

First a list of things I want.
Pearl chips in fish bowls,

pearl chips in bulb bowls.
Downtowns discontinued this product.

The policy approved by businesses today
is to suit production to employee.

Now a history of Valentines.
A woman in Worcester, Mass. —

Valentines were the passion of Esther's life,
but she lived and died unmarried.

Valentines were frowned on as "foolish notes,"
and the sending of them was forbidden.

Esther called in her girl-friend June
whose little caboose was Baby Beth.

June put a man on bathroom scales
in polka-dot shorts looking over his tummy.

June put a golfer with a golfball in a nest,
just to see how pretty they are underneath.

June wet her brushes in her mouth (tragic habit)
which led to her death by lead poisoning.

Times are hard on the Hi-desert,
studying visitors, flocks of mini-birds,

hanging upside-down on the suet-bags,
leaving in one grand rush.

Baby Beth, she too feels blue,
entertaining at a barbecue.

Yes, it's a small world I live in,
a warning system quite unique,

a zigzag path with different squares,
Doves in the Window, Broken Star,

a zigzag path with different squares,
Umbrella Girl, Broken Star, the both.

OCTOBER 29th

How would you like to see a great warm creature
large as a hill lumber towards you
to put a finger the size of a steeple on you

we left for the far reaches of the Smokies soon after
we stood the gum on a board, another gun on top — roof.
Bad birds! We stopped all the holes with glue.
The sills are tilted up to help the money stay put,
and at the bottom of each sill, you screw on a cap
that acts a a cushion so the money stays sealed.
Mud keeps out the moths with the tan abdomens.

Sixty thousand, living happily together in one family,
careering like a cyclone through the saliva of the stars,
careening like a typhoon among the lunar goobers.

The ancients used to believe if a baby in a cave
        angry father searching for him to kill him
        pockets stuffed with appalling personal possessions
if a baby rings bells or clashes tin pans in that cave
        anyway it all works out thus
        the bomb family is smaller
        than the ape family

46

P.M.

How would you like to see a little brown lady
with more eye-space than an owl, getting weaker
(takes a long tongue, a strong tongue to lap up sweetness —
that's why money doesn't run out as fast as it's put in)
the fields are the best place
to watch her put her tongue in the tubes

what's the matter with the clover
people say the bomb found an opening
but could only run its tongue along the outside
    began too late in life
    wandered too far from home
    to experiment and remember

we left for the nets in the fields soon after
and matted the grass over with nets
our white hairs turned a bright canary yellow
Setzt euch auf Rasen und grünes Gras
— sitting in the roses and the green green grass —
Whittier's written a poem about this. Read it.

NIGHT SOIL

Wrestled with smudges to attain the solar sheen you crave.
No reason in particular, except your wake-up wince,
and when you squint, can't see that violet network radiating outward
       (favorite childhood city) (eyeball) (rapid transit)
       (drugged caper of spaced-out spider) (Chicago)
       (flashlight suspended from ceiling) (euphoria hub)
which gives that feeling of well-being that means business is good.

Harangue: a new sky glares at us,
perforated by some authority or other's scent nozzles.
Perennial emergency, fuck off!
Then something South of France-ish to taper off to,
lemon verbena sifting down.
Rancid. Muttered: rancid.

Fledglings clomp about on the fire-escapes,
fire-escapes leading to and from silly heights,
heights designed to crumple inside a bag filled with lunar air,
air that insures perpetual nights with lots of sterile glitter.
Thus non-seeing organisms can really relax and trust stuff,
even the sodden slap slap slap of ephemera battling to get in,
persistent as a lazy lagoon bespangled orange twice a day,
orange as those distant relations, half-seen, half-sieve,
who don't realize how low the lowlands are,
lowlands that vent a dapper dullness,
the epitome of summer's end.

Warm farm weather's tarnishing the sky this time.
I love it when weather's like a speedboat in a lucky scene
in which pieces bob along, having perky tantrums,
tantrums because that windbreaker's zipper's a speck,
but if the light turns orange again,
it may be it's a lane
leading tractor onto plane.

Mere nostrums in the dusty brains of rusty men,
ready to leave these binds, egged on by a dogged with-it feeling,
feeling that a chunk of wood under dried grass (under snow)
by dint of sheer mattedness culls from the shadows
shadows that bounce from stone to stone.

A distant waterfall dumps rumblings on deaf lovers,
dear lovers, dead lovers. Rainy season's begun.

At entrance, pensioner sips beer. Little prissy thoughts.
Sneaky gas tamps down too-too raunchy udder draughts.
Another epitome of summer's end.

Another epitome of summer's end:
laser beams accelerating in operating rooms
papered over with derisive in-a-puny-time tits,
atchoo, atchoo, they fly shrieking into the air,
darkening the sky like a rain cloud
just to scratch some no longer obscene epithet on the one source of light,
as one might dirty a swank motel-room's white ruthlessness
till the last temporary wall has made itself scarce.

SMALL SODA

in my pants
ribbons of ennui
to undermine strangers
moving behind
throbbing hands

SINGLE

This magic weed is weird,
a long slow awakener.
Crazy Angel tapped with his fingers,
tapped at the mound. Ow!
Shared a beefsteak, so understanding,
(grow, my darlings, grow)
so motherly for a slow awakener.

CHINESE CREEP

for Harry Mathews

Reading Railroad. Gives a sigh
twice a day. Twice a day.

Gas girls, a set of hymns
dancing on the ceiling.

Precious little palaver.
Clean lion enters.

Cuss calls out to hoss: "Monument!"
Two minutes wait minute Two.

Shadowy nickels and quarters and dimes —
the big stiff.

Drastic variables:
so much lava, Fatso.

Rose. Then rose-colored. It's the Chinese Creep,
shadowy as the room into which he merges.

Clamber into your ump apparel fast.
Tring! Don't smell the bed, Bub.

Feel small and bombed today: lenient.
Liable to spell

last breath
fast birth.

An ominous gritting of the teeth
gumbo in a dirigible

thought he said: attack of miasma.
Referring to my asthma.

Damn mess.
In the stratosphere, same old fakery.

Reading Railroad, sometimes stresses
are afraid to wait too long — they get fizzy.

Then I feel loved in the altogether,
then I mean business. You get engaged, wham,

it's so precarious. Rose-colored liquids
redden the rain, Tlooth liquids.

Tlooth. Tlooth.
Scleam. Scleam.

No one will hear you but the hungly lats.
Something for which there's no sob-sister.

So much exhaust in this mattress.
In this pillow, silent stone hair.

LARRY'S SAVVY WAD

seven men sat
Zircon Circle

very low in their awareness
couldn't dent the little bus

uh, up, us
up, us, uh

women and chicks
maimed in the bedroom

lips jokingly practicing smacking
where am I now I need me

no lace
no nothing

just pure
lemon

lime
azure

come in and poke
The Great South

plump coral
white floral

violet
smoulder

SATIE FOR TWO

for Trevor Winkfield

girl comes out
gapes
man lying down
    panel opens

girl comes out
gapes
man lying down
     entanglements

panel opens
city people
impenetrable in all the right places
  science-fictiony

hide hands
armpits
between legs
    anywhere, anywhere

stale areas
can't have sex
under tension
    people must react

walk over side
beautiful field
flowers
  a reflash

GIRL MACHINE

my nerves my nerves I'm going mad
my nerves my nerves I'm going mad
round-the-world
hook-ups
head lit up   head lit up   head lit up
the fitting, the poodle
Ma Marine   Ma Marine   Ma Marine
Ma Marine   Ma Marine   Ma Marine
the fitting, the poodle

what a life,   just falling in and out of
what a life,   just falling in and out of
swimming pools
zylophones   WANTED   zylophones
WANTED female singer   WANTED
bigtime floorshow   bigtime floorshow
bigtime floorshow   bigtime floorshow
silhouetted in
moonlight
moonlight

mysterious mirrors
mysterious mirrors
mysterious mirrors

Louella Parsons

swell teeth	not news	swell teeth
"woo-woo"	woo-woo	"woo-woo"
vaccinated at 6 o'clock		in San Die
vaccinated at 6 o'clock		in San Die
"woo-woo"	woo-woo	"woo-woo"
swell teeth	not news	swell teeth

Louella Parsons

shiny black surfaces
shiny black surfaces
shiny black surfaces

head lit up   head lit up   head lit up
a girl machine
a girl machine
head lit up   head lit up   head lit up

```
work work work     work work work
work work work     work work work
work work work     work work work
work work work     work work work


GIRL MACHINE  GIRL MACHINE
GIRL MACHINE  GIRL MACHINE
GIRL MACHINE  GIRL MACHINE
```

"Busby Berkeley is the only film dir
"Busby Berkeley is the only film dir
to have fully experienced and re
to have fully experienced and re
Babe Rainbow   Babe Rainbow
Babe Rainbow   Babe Rainbow
signed Kenward G. Elms
signed Kenward G. Elms
mirrors provide a 2-
mirrors provide a 2-
for-1 opulence (D
for-1 opulence (D
epression /flo
epression /flo
wers: shit
wers: shit

wers: shit
wers: shit
on from above
on from above
bunches unfolding
bunches unfolding
in his "Footlight Par
in his "Footlight Par
signed Kenward G. Elms
signed Kenward G. Elms
Babe Rainbow   Babe Rainbow
Babe Rainbow   Babe Rainbow
beautiful people working for us!!
beautiful people working for us!!
"Busby Berkeley is the only film dir
"Busby Berkeley is the only film dir

GIRL MACHINE GIRL MACHINE
GIRL MACHINE GIRL MACHINE
GIRL MACHINE GIRL MACHINE

show gets on   and   is a smasheroo
show gets on   and   is a smasheroo
              round-the-world
                  hook-ups
head lit up   head lit up   head lit up
head lit up   head lit up   head lit up
     Ruby   Ruby
              col "yum" nist
(1969) BABE RAINBOW (1969)
            a girl machine
         reflected and refracted
by black floors   &   mystery meers
by black floors   &   mystery meers
Night in Shanghai Night in Shanghai

GIRL MACHINE GIRL MACHINE
GIRL MACHINE GIRL MACHINE
GIRL MACHINE GIRL MACHINE

lips painted red   lips painted red
keep on doing it   keep on doing it
        the oriental fans part
distant hands . . .   . . . distant hands
they come nearer   they come nearer
harmonica player   harmonica player
        creepy Chink beggars
whores kiss Dick   whores kiss Dick
falls for Jane Wy   falls for Jane Wy
pursued by gangs   pursued by gangs
        carries her shot dead
down a shadowy endless Dream Corridor!
harmonica player   harmonica player
they get smaller!   they get smaller!
distant hands . . .   . . . distant hands
        the oriental fans close

        42nd St.   42nd St.
        42nd St.   42nd St.
        reflected and refracted
by black floors and mystery meers
        reflected and refracted
        42nd St.   42nd St.
        42nd St.   42nd St.

you in the view and no real walls
you in the view and no real walls
express flow   black-whi
express flow   black-whi
          firm shiny terror
          firm shiny terror
express flow   black-whi
express flow   black-whi
you in the view and no real walls
you in the view and no real walls

GIRL MACHINE.   GIRL MACHINE.
GIRL MACHINE.   GIRL MACHINE.
GIRL MACHINE.   GIRL MACHINE.

          bunches
      like   flowers
down the ramp   down the ramp
happy factory   happy factory
just relax   just relax

TERRIFIC AFTERNOON

terrific afternoon
1970
Rose Bowl

blue fuse
took out cock
Sioux rock-pile

JUNK FISH

Selfish beast, wooden under the silk sheet.
More hum, more hum sun, more hum sun trudging
to Vienna, Vienna's sighs, Vienna's miserly treats:
    zircons filled with translucent liquid.

converted

       the beautiful dumb peninsula

into a white picket fence

to scarify

       extra-sensory made-in-Llasa

suction cups

siphoning up

	from back aways	
	grass	G
	prairie dog	E
	War dance	N
	dust	T
	gold	S

GENTS

back aways

       when each prearranged gusher's

ups had ups

now Marcel Duchamp

        discovers passport foto

of urinal in dead man's crotch

the real story

      begins just outside

Homeville

on Rain Goddess

        with purple prick big as
             Rockies   G
          chihuahuas   E
        tumbleweed   N
              smack   T
          implosion   S

GENTS

set: picturesque out-house

        camouflaged lab (?)

set on stucco hill: PATIO HILL

poisonous schoolmarm tsk-tsk-tsks

                                   bubble up

(Rain Goddess reincarnation) through the gulch

part club soda

                  part shudder

part Boom Time

covered over (more camouflage)

                            (laser beam germs)

with "organic" triple-action "kelp": mulch?

hey you guys

                  don't take a leak on that leaf

or (paroxysm) — I'm — I'm —

want to be around

                to see fleets of black boob zeppelins

hiding the crummy parts

junkies tinkering

              with old think tank

got-it-got-it-got-it-got-it gongs

gov't honky milk

             splatting down

on leaky long-buried cylinders' farts

snaking into my mouth

                like a slow-motion whip

with S&M thongs

GENE POOL

sample: elevator smells of dowager dust
press it into service sideways as mausoleum
inside it codicils set into motion
olden time programs that'll never terminate

sample: stagecoach jammed with wild-type cowboys
gabbing of condominiums in cornfields
which led to mobile mausoleums
which led to flying in the big buildings sideways

with machines to project soft walls inside
in case you want to feel up your neighbors
that and movie cartridges you pop in the oven
come dinner-time you can climb in too

lunch of shellfish stew
then it's out into the world
plate-glass coated with silver mirrors
exciting light impinging on fixed remains

zeroes and ones in twos and threes
all part of the pace
black and slanted (back and forth)
whipping past given points

MOTOR DISTURBANCE

Could be inching my way across moth turbulence
(wrong country? Honduras? — No! No! Nepal!)
due to a motor disturbance in some itinerary program computer
that failed to take into account my aversion to hot weather decay

and my love of eternal white silence
the result of a motor disturbance of some solar slope
I keep sliding down thanks to my own personal motor disturbance
the one that makes me puff up and screech (dog stars)

when I'd rather celebrate a White Cliff Mass
with friendly co-innocents in a clean commune above the clouds
where I won't have to cerebrate how to — how to — rip up stuff
work-oriented ancients painstakingly mass-produced

in vast sheets of legible shimmering matter
inspired, don't you know, by a longitude-latitude motor disturbance
(Earth plunges into new electro-magnetic black space field) —
exhausting! I can't control my current motor disturbance —

so clicky, soppy, so picky — like the one that led me to assume
"disfunction" was Brooklynese for "wedding" (nervous laughter)
which prompted me to dial NERVOUS first thing today
seeing as my booster clock . . . burnt oasis . . . plastic goo

so much of it this time of — of —
the operator's voice was laden with irony
irony I have no time to savor
due to the motor disturbance of this end-of-year period

which seems to be hurtling down a sleety dynamo
throbbing with hallucinatory instructions
each syllable of which lasts out a year of its own choosing
thanks to a blessed motor disturbance in the Heavens

i.e. your lips, gills, hills, tips —
a very contemporary motor disturbance as gorgeous as blue plates
spinning and wobbling and falling
conjoining to form Sky, replacing the old peeling one . . .

Sometimes you must persevere in the face of a huge motor disturbance
that settles on a whole city's brain like a big black bowl
part of an everywhere-in-the-universe night
like the one I see when the two mountains wrestling each other lie down

which happened in my mind just as I careened into your arms by mistake
to wish you a half-gnawed ear (new motor disturbance, I hate you!)
to wish you a Happy New Year Times (got it right for once)
and Happy New Year Times is my favorite motor disturbance of all

next to you who can transform stalled traffic into a beautiful panora —
(never get to finish this word in this particular lifetime)
ma — ma — a mama of endless blinky fields
with unicorns that honk as they twine around each other with languorous etc.

thanks to a permanent motor disturbance
just like mine, like yours, like ours, like our ecstasy
the ecstasy we left our nation in our will
to help it shudder its way through its inventive mole-run

the one its machines invented due to their one great motor disturbance,
the one that was supposed to prevent all the others,
the others that make me unable to figure out why
there's not one motor disturbance in the January sky

and in the winter air
with you there
everything in my life just seems to jell,
farewell.

GREAT EASTERN

In Lead, S.D.
    the first neutral organelle
        ate through its coolant jacket.
            77 Degrees Kelvin and in August.

Argon's capture rate dropped to zero,
    endangering the proton chain.
        Neutral organelles proliferated (gel)
            undetected in their muon disguise.

Astante! Antimony! Europium!
    The isotope "baron" arrived, enfeebled.
        10,000,000,000,000,000 lattice spacings —
            free paths for the Golgi Bodies.

K Minus Meson's chromosomal dregs
infiltrated Saturated Arc 28:
fungi (rust) on personal transit units.
The amino acid sequence began.

Propelled into the Crab Nebula
  safely inside the pulsar they slept.
    Metamorphosis. The screwworm flies
      crawled through the now diseased conduits,

while IB reminisced of argon-argon curves,
  ion-ion potentials, shell-shell interactions.
    "Aerial steamships to California"
    "the attachment of wings to balloons in still air"

"The great *Great Eastern* is laying a cable"
  "signals to the shore are well-nigh perfect" —
    IB was engrossed in visionary scenery.
    Leaks issued forth, the color of port.

The amino acid sequence was complete.
The vegemen phased themselves out.
Peroxisome injections! 8 Degrees Kelvin in May.
IB felt peppy as the oceans rose.